AN ADVENTURER'S GUIDE TO OUTER SPACE

WRITTEN BY
ISABEL THOMAS

FOREWORD BY
LUCY HAWKING

ILLUSTRATED BY
YAS IMAMURA

SPACE EXPLORER

LADYBIRD BOOKS

Ladybird Books is part of the Penguin Random House group of companies whose addresses can be found at global.penguinrandomhouse.com.

www.penguin.co.uk   www.puffin.co.uk   www.ladybird.co.uk

Penguin
Random House
UK

First published 2020

001

Foreword copyright © Lucy Hawking, 2020

Text by Isabel Thomas

Illustrations by Yas Imamura

Consultants: Stuart Atkinson and Dr Suzanne Imber

Copyright © Ladybird Books Ltd, 2020

Printed in China

A CIP catalogue record for this book is available from the British Library

ISBN: 978–0–241–36070–5

All correspondence to:
Ladybird Books, Penguin Random House Children's
One Embassy Gardens, New Union Square
5 Nine Elms Lane
London SW8 5DA

CONTENTS

BOARDING PASS

Foreword

Imagine you are standing on Planet Earth, looking up at the night sky. Perhaps you can see the face of the friendly Moon shining down on you. You might be able to see bright points of light, some of which are moving. They could be satellites – or perhaps the International Space Station, orbiting Earth while astronauts look out at our beautiful blue green home! If you know where to look, you might even see the giant planet of Jupiter. Further still are the stars, those flaming balls of gas that send light from trillions of miles away.

This book will take you on the most exciting adventure into space with Mia, travelling outwards until you reach . . . I won't tell you. You need to experience the journey for yourself!

Good luck on your cosmic travels – and remember, space is a dangerous place. So buckle up, stick with Mia and let's be on our way!

Lucy Hawking

Earth in space

Earth is a rocky ball wrapped in a blanket of air.
The air is invisible, but it keeps us safe and warm.
Beyond this blanket, far above our heads, is outer space.

Every day, the Sun lights up the Earth. Sunlight is a mixture
of every colour that you see in a rainbow.

Sunlight gets bounced about as it travels through Earth's blanket of air. Blue light gets bounced about more than other colours, so more of it reaches our eyes. This makes the sky look blue.

Time to go!
Are you ready for
an adventure?

Space adventure

Close this book and wave it through the air in front of you. On Earth, the book pushes the air out of the way. You can feel the air pushing back. In outer space, you would not feel anything as you moved the book. This is because there is almost no air in outer space.

Even if you stacked 50,000 fire engine ladders one on top of the other, then climbed all the way up, you would still find tiny wisps of air floating about.

There is no line to show where space starts, so we have to imagine one! This imaginary line is called the Kármán line and it is about 100 kilometres above Earth's surface.

KÁRMÁN LINE

The air gets thinner the higher you go. At the top of the highest mountain in the world, the air is so thin that breathing is difficult.

Earth's air is thickest near the ground. You can feel it rushing in and out of your nose as you breathe.

7

Looking into space

Outer space is mostly cold and dark, but you can see amazing things from Earth if you look up at the night sky.

It might seem as though the stars disappear during the day, but they don't. They just become harder to see. This is because the Sun's light is so incredibly bright that it hides the light of dim, faraway stars.

Look at the beautiful starry sky! Not every dot of light you see is a star. We can see six planets from Earth without even using a telescope!

A long time ago, people grouped the brightest stars together into shapes that are easy to remember, such as a unicorn, a scorpion, a dragon and a bear. These are called constellations.

Space adventure

On a dark, clear night, go outside with an adult. Look at the constellations shown at the very front and back of this book. Can you spot any of the constellations in the sky? How many can you see?

Before starlight reaches our eyes, it travels through the blanket of air that surrounds Earth. This bends the beams of light from faraway stars so that they seem to twinkle.

The ground feels firm under your feet, but Earth is always spinning in space. This is why the Sun seems to move across the sky during the day, and why the stars seem to move across the sky at night. In fact, it's Earth that is moving.

9

Leaving our planet

Gravity makes it hard to get into outer space. We have to use very powerful rockets to lift things into space.

When you throw a ball into the air, an invisible force called gravity pulls it back down to Earth. If you give the ball a bigger push by throwing it harder, it will travel a bit faster and get a bit higher, but gravity will still pull it back down again. To beat gravity, you need an enormous push – the kind that can only come from a rocket.

It doesn't take long to get into space – we'll be there in a few minutes.

Rockets are long, thin and pointy to help them move through the air more easily.

3. Sometimes, parts of the rocket are designed to fall away when their job is complete. Some fall back to Earth. Others stay in space.

2. At first, the rocket moves slowly. As the engines push the rocket into the sky, it moves faster and faster.

1. At take-off, most of the rocket is filled with oxygen and fuel. Huge engines burn the fuel, making lots of hot gas. The gas rushes out through nozzles at the bottom of the rocket. This pushes the rocket in the opposite direction – straight up!

Space adventure

Find somewhere with lots of room for you to move around. Then, put this book down and see how fast you can move away from it! How far can you move in one second? Ask someone to time you. Are you as fast as a rocket?

In one second . . .
• a car on a motorway travels 31 metres.
• the world's fastest train travels 167.5 metres.
• the world's fastest aeroplane travels 980 metres.
• a rocket leaving Earth's gravity travels 11,200 metres.

Orbiting Earth

If something is orbiting the Earth, it is travelling round and round the planet, high above our heads.

The International Space Station is the biggest spacecraft orbiting Earth. It zooms around the planet once every 90 minutes.

The space station is about 400 kilometres above Earth. Up here, the pull of gravity is almost as strong as it is down on the ground. This means that the station is always falling back to Earth – but it moves so fast that it just falls all the way round the planet!

Astronauts on the space station can zoom about and do somersaults in mid-air. This is called microgravity. You feel it on Earth when you drive over a little hill or whizz down a rollercoaster.

Space adventure

Hold this book out in front of you. Can you hold it in one hand? What would happen if you let go?

If you let go of the book on the International Space Station, it would float away in microgravity. You could even tap it backwards and forwards with just your fingertip!

There are usually six astronauts living and working on board the station at a time.

On-board machines collect and clean the water from the astronauts' wee, breath and sweat. This means they can drink the same water over and over again.

The International Space Station travels so fast that the astronauts see sixteen sunrises and sixteen sunsets every 24 hours!

Walking in space

Hundreds of astronauts have made the trip into orbit. There is warm air inside the space station, so the astronauts can wear normal clothes. When they go outside, they have to wear spacesuits.

A trip outside the space station is called a spacewalk. In sunlight it can be hotter than boiling water, while in the shade it is much colder than a freezer. The astronauts' suits help to keep them safe.

A spacewalk can last hours, so astronauts wear a type of large nappy!

Tubes of water are sewn into the spacesuit to keep the astronaut cool.

The suit is white so that some of the sunlight bounces away. Even the helmet has a shiny gold layer to stop the sunlight hurting the astronaut's face and eyes.

Astronauts wear bulky gloves and boots to stop their hands and feet getting too cold.

A spacesuit has more than eleven layers. On Earth, it weighs more than two grown-ups, but in microgravity it feels much lighter.

Space adventure

A spacesuit needs to keep the astronaut both alive and comfortable on their spacewalk. Some suits even have a patch of Velcro inside the helmet so that the astronaut can scratch an itch on their face!

Imagine you are going on a spacewalk for several hours. What would you want your spacesuit to include?

Look at the astronaut's spacesuit on this page and decide where to add each feature.

The Moon

The Moon is almost as old as Earth itself. It is covered in tall mountains, deep craters and a thick layer of grey dust.

The Moon doesn't make its own light. Moonlight is really sunlight that has bounced off the Moon towards Earth, a bit like a giant mirror in the sky.

There is no wind or weather on the Moon. The footprints of visiting astronauts will stay in the dust for millions of years.

Every year, the Moon moves about 4 centimetres further away from Earth.

```
0    1    2    3    4
|cm|....|....|....|....|
```

The Moon is the furthest from Earth that humans have ever been. Astronauts have walked, bounced, driven a buggy and even played golf on the Moon!

Space adventure

People have always told stories about the pictures they see on the Moon's surface. These pages show how the Moon looks from the northern part of the world. Can you see the shape of a face? Can you spot any other pictures?

Now turn the book upside down.

This is how the Moon looks from the southern part of the world! Can you see a crab on the surface?

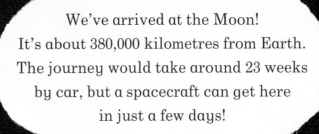

We've arrived at the Moon! It's about 380,000 kilometres from Earth. The journey would take around 23 weeks by car, but a spacecraft can get here in just a few days!

Spacecraft have been to the Moon and taken photos of the mountains and craters. They have discovered dark rocks that were once lava from volcanoes, and they have even spotted frozen water! This is exciting, because it means that humans might be able to build a base on the Moon one day.

Seen from Earth, the shape of the Moon appears to change each night. This is because the Sun only lights up one side of the Moon. As the Moon moves around Earth, we see different amounts of the sunlit side. We can't see the parts that are in darkness.

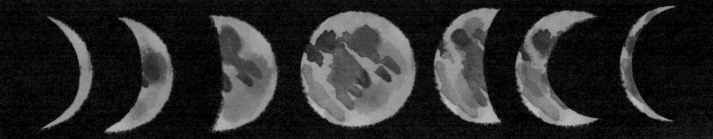

The Sun

The Sun is a star, but it's much closer to Earth than the other stars in the sky. Without the Sun, Earth would be dark and frozen.

All stars are fiery balls of hot gas. The Sun is only a medium-sized star, but it's close enough to Earth to light and heat our whole planet. Even from 150 million kilometres away, the Sun's energy can melt ice creams and burn our skin.

You should never look directly at the Sun! It is so bright, it would damage your eyes.

18

The Sun is wrapped in a thick, glowing cloud of gas called the corona. This makes it hard for spacecraft to get close to the Sun.

Light is the fastest thing in the universe. It takes about eight minutes for light to travel the 150 million kilometres from the Sun to Earth.

Sunspots are cooler, darker parts of the Sun's surface.

Space adventure

If the Moon moves between Earth and the Sun, it can block out the Sun's light. This is called a solar eclipse. Put this book down, then go to the other end of the room. Hold up your thumb and close one eye. Can you block out the book with your thumb, like an eclipse?

The Sun is 400 times wider than the Moon, but when we look up at the sky they seem to be about the same size. This is because the Sun is 400 times further away from us than the Moon.

Earth feels huge when you're a human standing on it, but it's tiny compared to the Sun. You could fit more than a million Earths inside the Sun!

For us on Earth, the Sun is the most important star in the whole universe.

Sometimes, there is a huge explosion called a solar flare. Solar flares are the hottest things in the Solar System.

Our Solar System

Mars

Mercury

Venus

Earth

ASTEROID BELT

A year is the amount of time it takes a planet to make one trip around the Sun. On Earth, this takes just over 365 days. Some planets take much longer than this, while others are quicker.

20

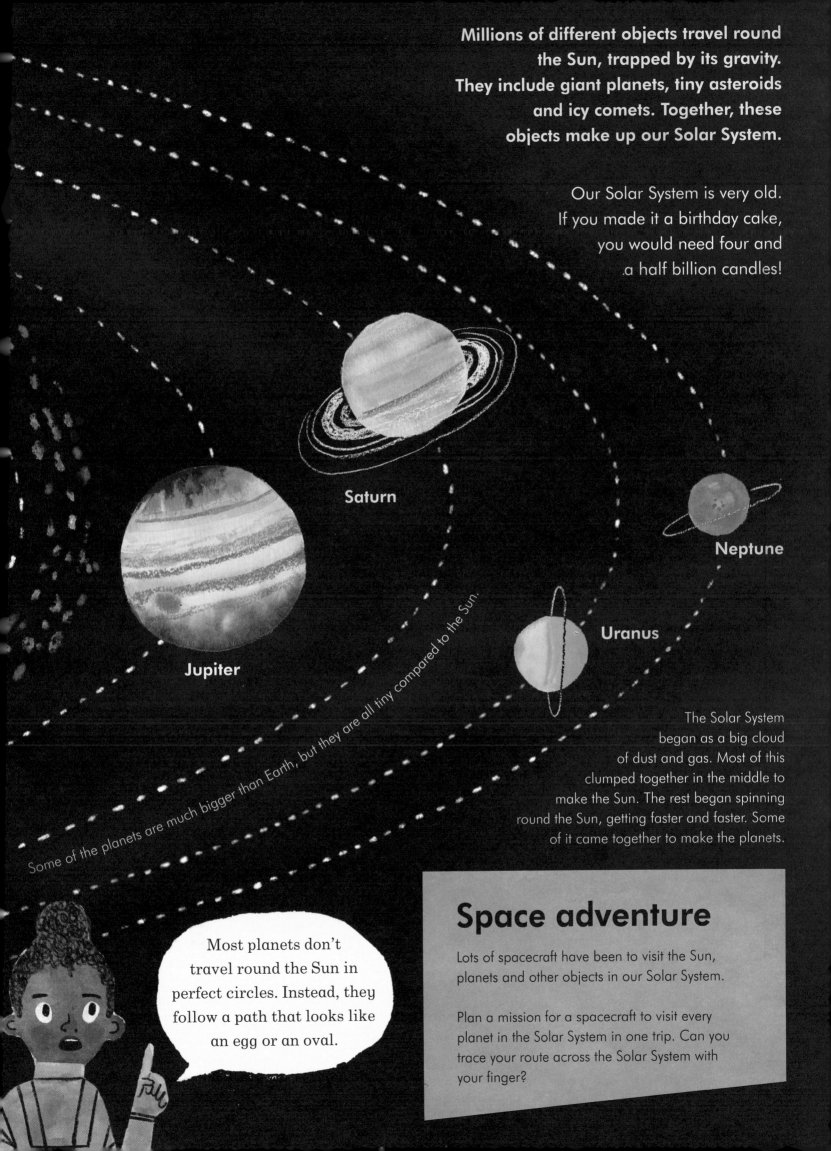

Millions of different objects travel round the Sun, trapped by its gravity. They include giant planets, tiny asteroids and icy comets. Together, these objects make up our Solar System.

Our Solar System is very old. If you made it a birthday cake, you would need four and a half billion candles!

Saturn

Neptune

Jupiter

Some of the planets are much bigger than Earth, but they are all tiny compared to the Sun.

Uranus

The Solar System began as a big cloud of dust and gas. Most of this clumped together in the middle to make the Sun. The rest began spinning round the Sun, getting faster and faster. Some of it came together to make the planets.

Most planets don't travel round the Sun in perfect circles. Instead, they follow a path that looks like an egg or an oval.

Space adventure

Lots of spacecraft have been to visit the Sun, planets and other objects in our Solar System.

Plan a mission for a spacecraft to visit every planet in the Solar System in one trip. Can you trace your route across the Solar System with your finger?

Mercury and Venus

Mercury and Venus are the planets closest to the Sun. Large areas of these planets are much hotter than anywhere on Earth.

Mercury is the smallest planet in our Solar System. It's only a little bigger than our moon, and its gravity is not strong enough to trap air.

Like the Moon, Mercury is covered in craters made by crashing space rocks.

Mercury and Venus zoom round the Sun more quickly than Earth does. A year on Mercury is just 88 Earth days long!

When it's daytime on Mercury, the Sun heats the ground to more than twice the temperature of an oven. At night, the heat escapes back into space and Mercury becomes twice as cold as Antarctica.

Mercury

If I landed on Mercury and looked out of my rocket window, the Sun would look about three times bigger than it does from Earth!

Space adventure

Put this book in the middle of a room with plenty of space to move around. Practise spinning slowly, like Mercury and Venus. Try to move in a circle around the book as you spin. You are now orbiting like a planet!

Venus and Earth are about the same size, but the air on Venus is much thicker. Standing on Venus would feel like diving deep underwater.

Venus takes 243 Earth days to spin round once. That's longer than it takes to travel around the Sun, so a Venus day is longer than a Venus year!

Venus

The thick air traps so much heat from the Sun that Venus is the hottest planet in the Solar System.

Venus's skies are always cloudy, and it's impossible to see through the thick clouds from space.

Mercury, Venus, Earth and Mars are called the rocky planets. They have solid rock surfaces that you could walk on.

thin layer of solid rock
melting rock
extremely hot metal

Mercury   **Venus**   **Earth**   **Mars**

Mars

Humans haven't been to Mars yet, but we have sent lots of robots to explore the red planet.

Billions of years ago, Mars was warmer and had rivers and lakes. Today, the ground is cold and dry, but one orbiter robot has discovered a huge, salty lake hidden deep underground.

Deimos

Mars looks red because it is covered with a thin layer of rust.

Phobos

Mars

Mars has two moons, and they are called Phobos and Deimos. These names mean "fear" and "terror", but the moons don't look scary. They look like lumpy boulders!

Mars may be the first planet that humans visit from Earth. Scientists are busy finding ways for astronauts to live on Mars. They have made soil just like the soil on Mars, and have grown tomatoes, peas, radishes and potatoes in it. These Mars vegetables were just as tasty as the ones grown in Earth soil!

Vehicles called rovers have driven across Mars's rocky red surface. They have taken photos, scooped soil and drilled into rocks. New rovers will look for fossils and other signs of ancient life on Mars.

A robot lander called InSight has been finding out what Mars is like on the inside. It can measure how much the ground shakes when big space rocks hit the surface. This is called a marsquake!

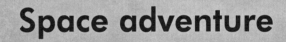

Space adventure

Driving a Mars rover is tricky. Engineers write instructions on Earth and beam them to Mars using radio. It takes up to 24 minutes for the instructions to travel all the way to Mars, so it is impossible for the rover to brake quickly!

With a friend, make a Mars-like landscape using cushions as rocks, craters and sand dunes. Take it in turns to be a Mars rover, while your friend is the engineer sending you instructions. Can you travel across Mars without getting stuck?

A day on Mars is called a sol. It is a bit longer than a day on Earth.

Asteroids, comets and meteorites

Planets and their moons aren't the only things that orbit the Sun. There are billions of smaller rocks zooming round the Solar System, too.

Asteroids are lumps of dusty rock. Millions of asteroids take the same path between Mars and Jupiter on their voyage round the Sun. This crowded path is called the asteroid belt.

Have you ever rolled a snowball that got covered in dust and gravel? If you kept rolling it until your dirty snowball was the size of a town, you would have made a comet!

Comet

Most comets are found in the darkest, coldest parts of the Solar System. Sometimes a comet zooms closer to the Sun. As it warms up, the ice begins to melt. This gives the comet a tail of gas and dust.

The largest asteroid is called 4 Vesta. Sometimes it can be seen in the sky from Earth without a telescope.

Anyone who discovers a new asteroid is allowed to name it. There are asteroids named after teachers, musicians and even a cat! There might be one that has your name.

Asteroid

Space adventure

Small space rocks and specks of comet dust hurtle towards Earth every year. As they zoom towards the ground, they rub against Earth's air. Rub your hands together quickly. Can you feel them getting warm? Meteors get so hot when they rub against Earth's air that they glow. They are shooting stars. On a clear night, go outside with a grown-up and see if you can spot any!

Meteorite

Most meteors burn up before they reach the ground. Space rocks that do land on Earth are called meteorites. They are usually no bigger than a speck of dust or a grain of sand. Big meteorites are very rare. Only the biggest make a crater when they land.

Meteor

Spacecraft have visited comets and asteroids, and even landed on them!

Jupiter

Jupiter is a giant! All of the other planets in the Solar System could fit inside Jupiter together.

Jupiter spins very quickly. A full day lasts ten hours – there are just five hours of daylight before it's night again.

Jupiter is mostly made of the same gases as the Sun, but it's not big enough to burn like the Sun.

Storms on Jupiter are much bigger than Earth's hurricanes. The Great Red Spot is a storm that's wider than our whole planet!

Jupiter spins so quickly that its thick clouds race and swirl around it. Jupiter looks stripy because the clouds move at different speeds.

> Planets and moons are all different colours because they are made of different things.

Space adventure

Jupiter's four largest moons are so big that you can see them from Earth with binoculars. If Jupiter's moons were as small as they are on this page, Mercury would be the size of a table tennis ball. Find a table tennis ball and put it down next to the moons below. What do you discover?

Ganymede is bigger than Mercury!

Jupiter has so many moons that it's hard to keep count. More than 50 have been named so far, and over 25 more have been spotted.

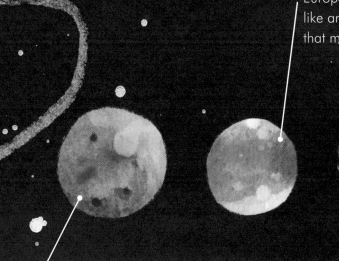

Europa
Europa's icy surface is covered in cracks, like an ice rink! Below the ice is an ocean that might be home to living things.

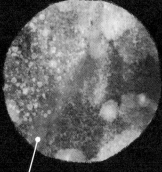

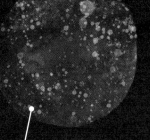

Io
Io is covered in fiery volcanoes. Lava erupts high into the sky and flows into lakes.

Ganymede
Ganymede is the largest moon in the Solar System.

Callisto
Callisto is almost the same size as Mercury. Its surface is covered in craters.

Jupiter and Saturn are gas giants. Uranus and Neptune are ice giants. They all probably have rocky centres, but they are mostly liquid and gas. Stepping on to one of these planets would be a bit like stepping into a cloud.

- clouds and gas
- liquid and ice
- ice and rock

Jupiter   **Saturn**   **Uranus**   **Neptune**

Saturn

Saturn often shines brightly in the night sky. Although it is ten times further from the Sun than we are, some of Saturn's secrets can be seen from Earth.

Like Jupiter, Saturn is mostly made of thick cloud. It looks calm and peaceful from space, but giant ice storms rage in the clouds.

Saturn has seven sparkling rings, but they aren't solid. Each one is made of billions of chunks of ice and rock that twinkle in the sunlight.

Saturn takes 29 Earth years to make its way round the Sun.

If you use a telescope, you can see Saturn's sparkling rings from Earth!

These chunks zoom round Saturn like cars on a motorway. Each ring goes at its own speed. Some of the chunks are small specks of dust. Others are as big as houses or even mountains!

Space adventure

Around twice every thirty years, Saturn's rings look almost invisible from Earth. This is because its rings are so thin that they are difficult to see when the planet tilts in a different direction. Hold this book out in front of you and tilt it backwards and forwards. Sometimes you can see the top of the book, and sometimes you can only see the edge!

Enceladus

Saturn has 82 moons. Enceladus is one of Saturn's moons. It would be a good place to look for aliens! It has a giant ocean of water covered with a layer of ice.

Saturn's rings are wide, but very thin. From the side, they are about 30 metres high – that's the same height as a tall tree.

As winds swirl about Saturn, they form a golden hexagon that spins round the top of the planet. Each side of the hexagon is wider than Earth!

Titan

With binoculars, you might be able to spot Saturn's biggest moon, Titan, from Earth.

Uranus and Neptune

These lonely, icy giants are famous for their strong winds and smelly clouds.

Both Uranus and Neptune are made from a slushy mix of water and other things. Some of the water is solid ice, but not because it's cold. It freezes because it's being squeezed so much by the planets' enormous gravity.

Neptune and Uranus both have clouds made of the same gas that gives sewage and rotten eggs their stinky smell!

Uranus

Uranus is the only planet that spins on its side. This makes its seasons very long. The north pole gets 21 years of night-time in winter, and 21 years of daytime in summer.

All of the giant planets have rings, but Jupiter, Uranus and Neptune's rings are very hard to see. They are made of tiny specks of dust and ice.

Since it is bright blue, Neptune was named after the Roman god of the sea. What other names can you think of for a bright blue planet?

Neptune is 30 times further from the Sun than Earth is. Sunlight can travel there in just over four hours, but it would take a car around 4,500 years to drive that far!

Neptune

Neptune has faster winds than any other planet. They swirl around the planet more than four times faster than the world's quickest sports car! This makes strange whirlpools in the planet's bright blue clouds.

It takes 156 Earth years for Neptune to make one trip round the Sun.

Pluto and the dwarf planets

The Solar System continues far beyond the planets. Way into the distance, billions of space rocks are slowly orbiting the Sun.

When Pluto was first discovered, it was called a planet. Then space scientists decided that Pluto was the wrong size and in the wrong orbit to be a planet. They called it a dwarf planet instead. As well as Pluto, four other dwarf planets have been spotted.

Ceres

Ceres is the closest dwarf planet to Earth. It travels around the Sun in the asteroid belt. A spacecraft has visited Ceres and discovered that it has lots of water.

The Sun

Venus

Mars

Earth

Mercury

Jupiter

The Solar System is enormous! The furthest edge of the Kuiper Belt is about 50 times further from the Sun than Earth is.

Haumea

Space adventure

The dwarf planets are all made of solid rock that you could walk and jump on. Since they are small, their gravity is much weaker than Earth's gravity. Try jumping in the air. How high can you go? On Pluto, you would be able to bounce nearly fifteen times higher, and you would stay off the ground for almost ten seconds!

Kuiper Belt

Pluto, Haumea, Makemake and Eris are all found in the Kuiper Belt (say *"kigh-per"*). This part of the Solar System is like a massive asteroid belt, but much further from the Sun.

Pluto

Uranus

Neptune

Saturn

Far beyond the Kuiper Belt is the Oort Cloud. This cloud may contain more than a trillion icy comets. It is like a shell around the Solar System.

Makemake

Eris

Stars

The stars are so far away that only a tiny part of their light reaches Earth. Most of the stars we can see from Earth are bigger than the Sun.

On a clear, dark night, we can see a few thousand of the brightest stars in the sky. Binoculars help us to see hundreds of thousands more, and with a telescope we can see millions!

Proxima Centauri is the nearest star to our Sun, but it is so far away that its light takes more than four years to reach Earth.

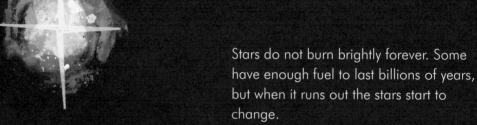

Stars do not burn brightly forever. Some have enough fuel to last billions of years, but when it runs out the stars start to change.

Small stars swell up, then shrink down and become cool and dim. One day, they stop shining altogether. This will happen to our Sun one day – but not for more than five billion years.

Massive stars don't fade away. They explode in a bright, colourful supernova. From Earth, a supernova looks like a huge, glowing star. Some are so bright that they can even be seen during the day.

Supernova

A supernova blasts parts of the star into space. This stardust becomes the building blocks for everything else in the universe – including us!

The parts of the old star that are left behind get pulled together by their own gravity. It's a bit like packing all of Earth into a space the size of a pea! The gravity of this tiny old star can become so strong that even light can't escape. This is called a black hole.

Space adventure

Look closely and you'll see that stars glow with different colours. The hottest stars are blue. The coolest stars are red. Stars in the middle glow white or yellow, like our Sun. Can you find blue, red, white and yellow stars in the picture?

Exoplanets

Many other stars have planets of their own. These are known as exoplanets, and they are not part of our Solar System.

Imagine a tiny insect crawling across a car headlight. The headlight would get slightly dimmer as the bug blocked the light. This is one way telescopes can spot exoplanets. The telescope looks at a star for a long time. If the light from the star gets dimmer, then brighter again, it's a clue that a planet is passing in front of the star.

Earth is a very special planet. It's not too hot, and it's not too cold. It's just right for living things. This is why planets like Earth are called Goldilocks planets! Space scientists are trying to find other planets that are just right for living things.

Space adventure

We might even find new planets in our own Solar System! Scientists have found clues that a huge Planet Nine is orbiting the Sun, further away than Pluto. Think about all the amazing planets you've discovered on this adventure. What might a new planet look like? Would you want to visit it?

Proxima b is an exoplanet that orbits the star Proxima Centauri. Proxima b would be a good place to look for aliens, but we won't be able to do this for hundreds of years, because it is so far away.

Not all planets orbit stars. Rogue planets drift around the Milky Way on their own. There are probably more rogue planets than there are stars, but they are very hard to spot.

Exoplanets are very exciting. Scientists think there could be many billions of exoplanets in our galaxy!

The Milky Way

Stars aren't evenly spaced across the universe. They cluster together in groups called galaxies. Our Solar System is part of a galaxy called the Milky Way.

A galaxy is an enormous group of billions of stars that are held together by gravity. The stars orbit the centre of the galaxy, just like planets orbit a star.

Our Sun is 26,000 light years from the centre of the Milky Way. The Sun zooms around the galaxy, taking everything in our Solar System along for the ride!

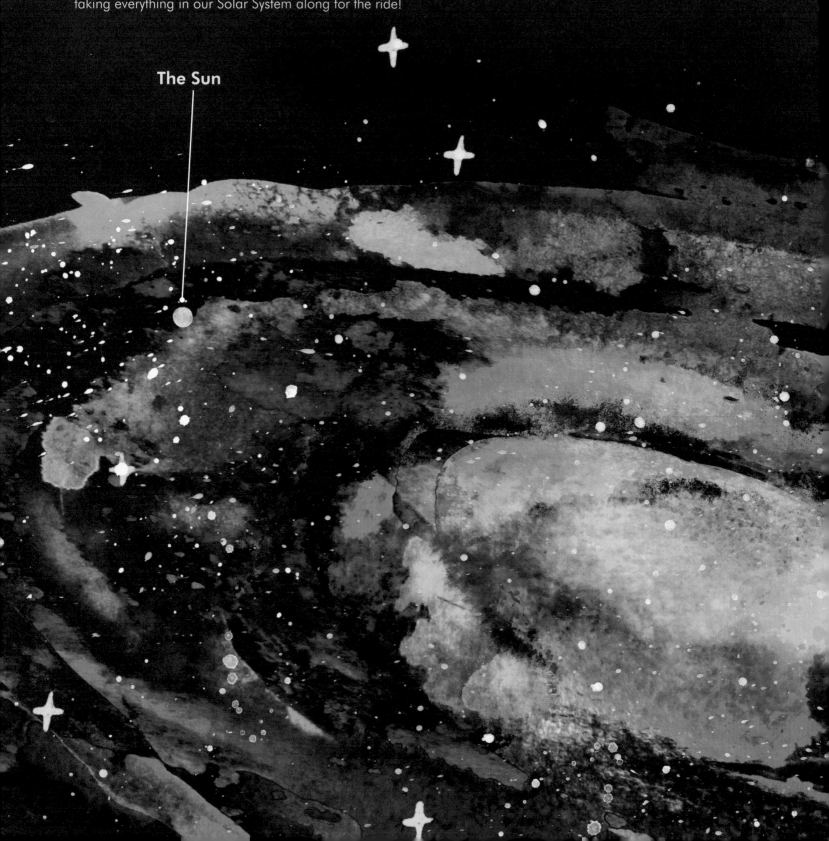

The Sun

Galaxies are much bigger than solar systems. The fastest spacecraft that humans have ever invented would take 40 million years to reach the centre of the Milky Way. If it did get there, it would find a black hole many times bigger than the Sun, surrounded by other stars.

The gaps between stars are not completely empty. In some places, there is a giant cloud of dust and gas, called a nebula. Sometimes, the dust and gas clump together. Their gravity gets stronger, pulling in more and more dust and gas. The cloud heats up and begins to glow. This is how new stars begin.

Space adventure

Lay this book on a flat surface, with these pages open. Spin the book round and round to see our Sun orbit the centre of the Milky Way.

The Milky Way is so big that each trip round it takes 230 million years. The last time our Solar System was in the position it is today, dinosaurs were living on Earth!

The Ancient Greeks and Romans thought the Milky Way looked like a road of milk across the sky!

We can't see the whole Milky Way from Earth, because we are part of it! When we look up at the night sky and see a misty band of stars, we are looking at the Milky Way.

Other galaxies

Almost everything you can see in the night sky is part of the Milky Way. On a very dark night, you might spot other galaxies, too.

Powerful telescopes can peer deep into space and take pictures of many more galaxies. The Hubble Space Telescope has created a picture that shows 15,000 different galaxies.

Billions of galaxies are scattered across the universe. From Earth, we can see a few without a telescope. The Magellanic Clouds are two nearby galaxies that are easy to spot from the southern half of Earth.

Some galaxies are ball-shaped or egg-shaped.

Spiral galaxies are shaped like our Milky Way. They have long arms of stars that curve round the centre. They look a bit like whirlpools.

No one has counted all of the stars in the universe, but we know that there must be more stars in the universe than grains of sand on all the beaches on Earth.

Space adventure

The 15,000 galaxies in the Hubble Space Telescope's picture are all in the same tiny patch of sky. There are thousands of galaxies in every other patch of sky, too, but they haven't been photographed yet.

Hold this book high above your head and look at the galaxies in the picture. Can you imagine the other galaxies all around you?

Some galaxies are just clouds of stars with no special shape at all.

Galaxies are grouped together in huge clusters. Some clusters contain millions of galaxies!

Galaxies have very strong gravity, and they can pull in smaller galaxies and grow even bigger. The Canis Major Dwarf Galaxy is the next-closest galaxy to Earth. It's being gobbled up by the Milky Way. One day, its billion stars will just be part of our galaxy.

The universe

The universe is the name for everything that exists. It includes Earth, the Sun, our Solar System, other stars, exoplanets and all the galaxies. It even includes things that we can't see.

Everything in the universe was once squashed into a space so tiny and hot that it's impossible to imagine. There was no space, and no time.

About fourteen billion years ago, everything inside this tiny dot suddenly began expanding. The universe began with this Big Bang.

As the universe got bigger and cooler, stars and galaxies began to form. Billions of years later, the universe is still expanding and changing.

44

Space adventure

We have only just begun exploring the universe. There is so much more to explain and discover. Look closely at the page. Which mysteries of the universe will you solve? What secrets will you discover?

When you stare up at the night sky, you are looking far across the universe. You might even see Andromeda, the nearest spiral galaxy to the Milky Way.

The light from Andromeda takes two million years to travel across space to your eyes. When you look at Andromeda, you are actually seeing what it looked like two million years ago, when the light began its journey towards us. You are looking back in time.

Our eyes can only see light. Scientists have invented telescopes that can see different types of rays, but there is still a lot out there that we can't see – including dark matter. It's invisible to our eyes and to telescopes, but we know it must be there because its gravity holds galaxies together.

All aboard! It's time to head back home.

45

That was an amazing voyage! Exploring outer space helps us to understand more about our place in the universe. Scientists, engineers, astronomers and astronauts are always finding new information about space, and there's still so much to discover! What will your adventure be?

Glossary

asteroid	a large rock, smaller than a planet, that orbits the Sun
Big Bang	a huge explosion that scientists believe created the universe
black hole	an area in space with such strong gravity that nothing can escape it
comet	an object usually made of ice and dust that can sometimes have a tail when it's near the Sun
constellation	a group of stars that form a pattern and have a name
corona	the layer of hot gas that surrounds the Sun
dwarf planet	a rocky object that orbits the Sun, but is not big enough to be a planet
exoplanet	a planet that is not in our Solar System
galaxy	an enormous group of stars and planets, like the Milky Way
gas giants	the name given to Jupiter and Saturn
gravity	the force that pulls things towards Earth, the Sun and other objects in space
ice giants	the name given to Uranus and Neptune
International Space Station	a space station that orbits Earth and is used as a science lab in outer space
Kármán line	the imaginary line where space begins – aeroplanes can only fly below it
Kuiper Belt	an area of the outer Solar System that is home to the dwarf planets Pluto, Haumea and Makemake
light year	the distance that light travels in one year
meteor	a piece of rock from space that glows brightly as it travels through Earth's air
meteorite	a piece of rock from space that has landed on Earth
microgravity	when people or objects seem to be weightless – like astronauts floating in space
Milky Way	the galaxy that contains our Solar System
moon	an object like a small planet that orbits a larger planet
nebula	a cloud of gas or dust in space
Oort Cloud	a thick shell of ice and rock that surrounds our Solar System
orbit	moving round an object, usually in a circular or oval-shaped path
planet	a large, round object made from rock, metal or gas that orbits a star
rocky planets	the name given to Mercury, Venus, Earth and Mars
rogue planet	a planet that does not orbit a star, and travels around the galaxy on its own
solar eclipse	when the Moon moves between the Sun and Earth, and blocks out the Sun's light for a few moments
solar flare	a big explosion that makes the Sun glow more brightly
solar system	a star and the planets, comets, asteroids and moons that travel round it
spacewalk	when an astronaut travels out of a spacecraft and moves around in outer space
star	a giant ball of burning gas in space
sunspots	dark, cool patches on the surface of the Sun
supernova	an old star exploding
universe	everything in outer space, including the planets, the stars and all of us